Now That's What I Call

COLOUR ME GOOD
RECORD SLEEVES 2

Mel Elliott

Published by I Love Mel
© Mel Elliott 2014
ISBN: 978 0 9927777 8 4
Printed in the UK

Madonna
Madonna

Warner Bros, 1982
Artwork: Carin Goldberg
Photograph: Gary Heery

Miley Cyrus
Wrecking Ball

RCA, 2013
Photography: Terry Richardson

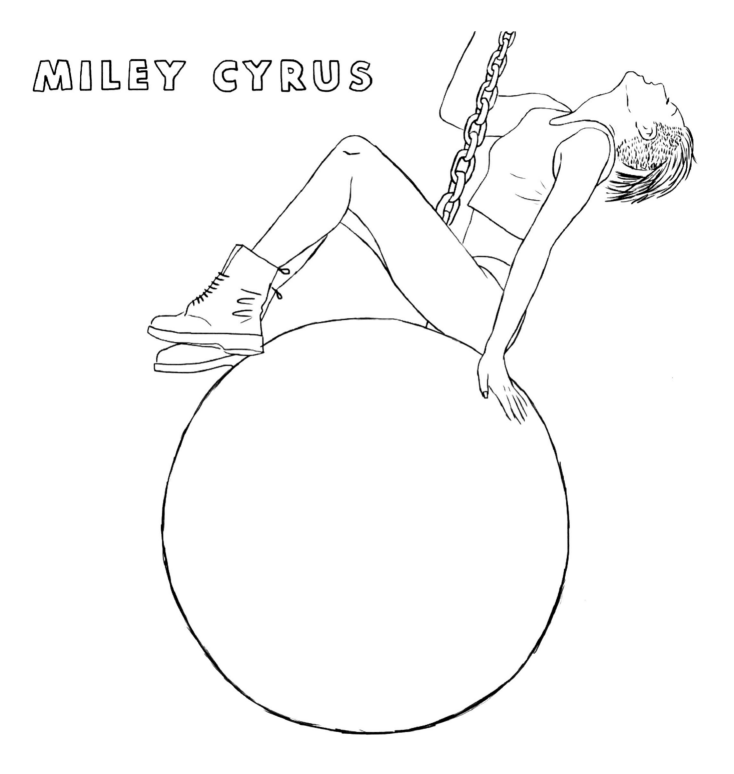

Nirvana
Nevermind

Geffen, 1991
Artwork: Robert Fisher
Photograph: Kirk Weddle

Taylor Swift
We Are Never Ever Getting Back Together

Big Machine, 2012

The Doors
The Best Of The Doors

Compilation Album
Elektra, 1985
Photograph: Joel Brodsky

Grace Jones
Slave To The Rhythm

Manhattan Records, 1985
Artwork/Design: Jean-Paul Goude

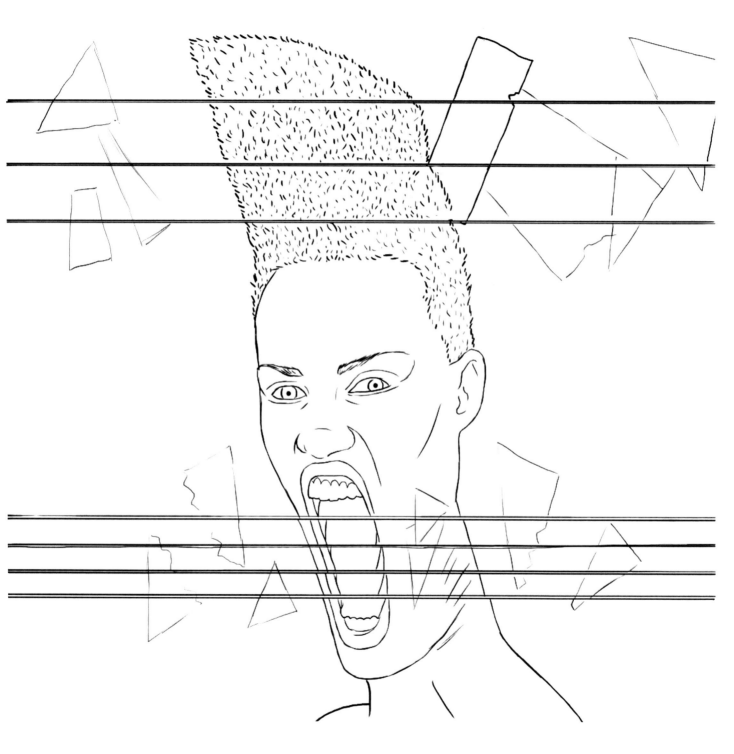

Michael Jackson
Thriller

Epic, 1982
Sleeve Photography: Dick Zimmerman

Michael Jackson
Thriller

Lana Del Rey
Born To Die

Interscope, Polydore, 2012
Sleeve Photography: Nicole Nodland

Jake Bugg
Jake Bugg

Mercury, Island, 2012

Blondie
Denis

Compilation Album
EMI, 1996

Simon & Garfunkel
Bookends

Columbia, 1968
Sleeve Photography: Richard Avedon

BOOKENDS/SIMON & GARFUNKEL

Whitney Houston
Whitney

Arista, 1987
Sleeve Photography: Richard Avedon

Eminem
The Marshall Mathers LP 2

Aftermath, Shady, Interscope, 2013
Art Director/Design: Jason Noto

Patti Smith
Horses

EMI, 1975
Sleeve Photography: Robert Mapplethorpe

Patti Smith Horses

The Strokes
Is This It

RCA 2001
Sleeve Photography/Design: Colin Lane

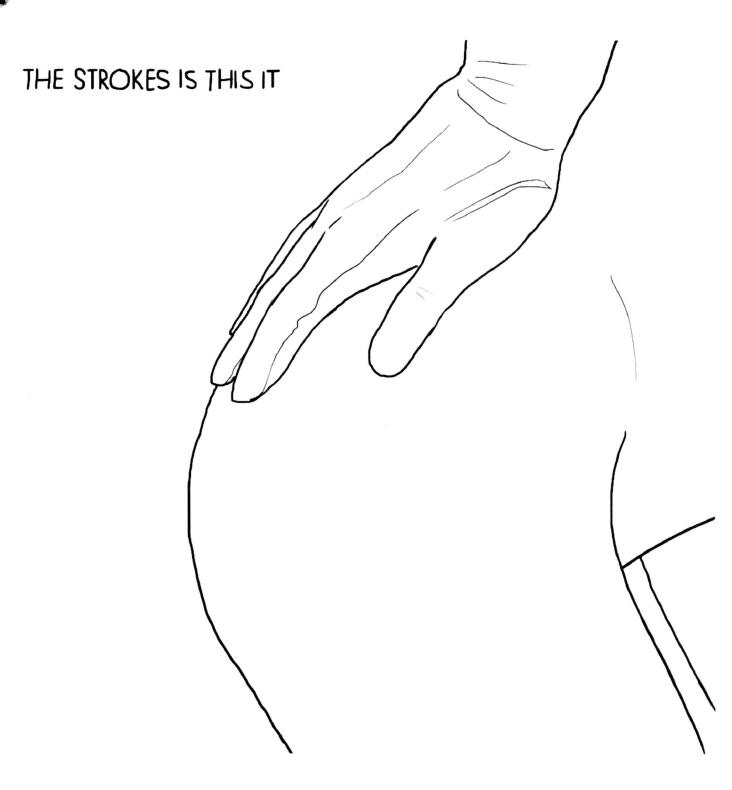

PLEASE SHOW ME YOUR COLOURING IN:
ON INSTAGRAM: I_LOVE_MEL
OR ON TWITTER: @MELLYELLIOTT

JOIN IN WITH COLOUR ME GOOD THURSDAYS!
GET YOUR FELT-TIPS OR PENCILS OUT AND
JUST USE THE HASHTAG #CMGT

Distributed in the United States and Canada by SCB Distributors.
Distributed outside of the United States and Canada by Turnaround Publisher Services.